DECODABLE BOOK 24

Orlando   Boston   Dallas   Chicago   San Diego

Visit *The Learning Site!*
www.harcourtschool.com

Copyright © by Harcourt, Inc.

All rights reserved. No part of this publication may be reproduced or transmitted in any form or by any means, electronic or mechanical, including photocopy, recording, or any information storage and retrieval system, without permission in writing from the publisher.

Requests for permission to make copies of any part of the work should be addressed to School Permissions and Copyrights, Harcourt, Inc., 6277 Sea Harbor Drive, Orlando, Florida 32887-6777. Fax: 407-345-2418.

HARCOURT and the Harcourt Logo are trademarks of Harcourt, Inc., registered in the United States of America and/or other jurisdictions.

Printed in the United States of America

ISBN 0-15-326704-6

11 12 13 179 10 09 08 07 06 05

Ordering Options
ISBN 0-15-323767-8 (Collection)
ISBN 0-15-326738-0 (package of 5)

Contents

Howdy Clown 1
Variant Vowel /ou/*ow*

What Joan Found 9
Variant Vowel /ou/*ou*

Bow-Wow Hound 17
Variant Vowel /ou/*ow*

The Grouchy Mice 25
Variant Vowel /ou/*ou*

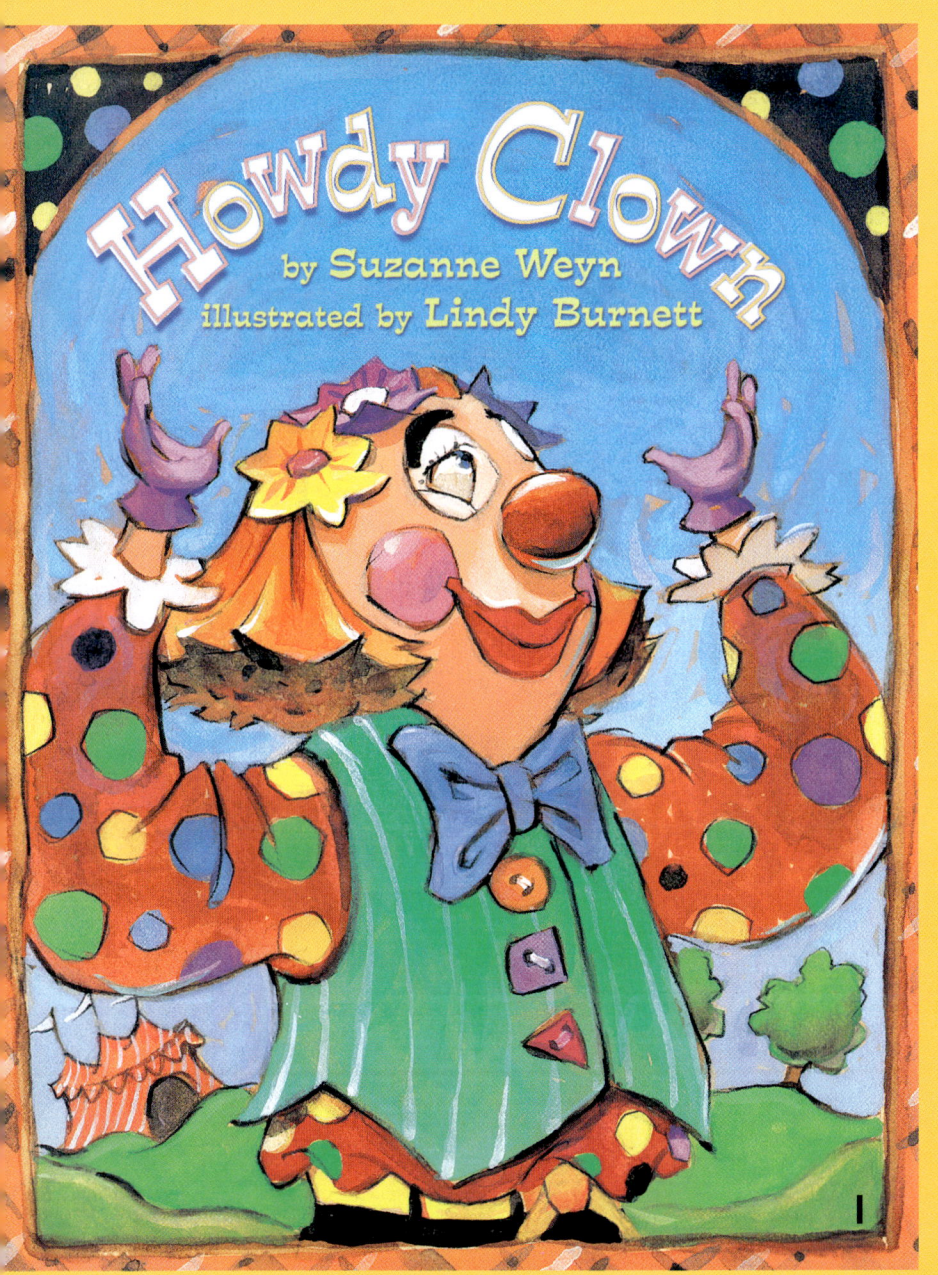

She looks up
and sees a smile.
It makes her giggle
all the while.

She looks down
and sees red lips.
"Just what I need,"
Howdy yips.

She slaps the lips
upon her face.
She frowns and growls
all around the place!

Now Howdy Clown
is feeling sad.
Now Howdy Clown
is feeling bad.

She flips her lips upside down.

Now Howdy smiles.
She doesn't frown!

What Joan Found

by Nancy Furstinger
illustrated by Anthony Lewis

Hush!
Don't shout. Don't make a sound.
Joan is digging in the ground.

Joan is digging. She's made a mound.
Joan found something in the ground.

Joan is crouching down to see.
She found some bugs near the tree!

Joan tickles a bug.
It curls up and gets small.
The bug curls up
in a round, round ball.

The round ball tumbles down the mound.
It rushes back into the ground.

"Dad!" Joan whispers.
"Don't make a sound.
What kind of bugs have I found?"

"They are sow bugs.
That's what you found.
Sow bugs like the damp, wet ground."

Bow-Wow Hound

by Nancy Furstinger
illustrated by Dan Sharp

Bow-Wow Hound trots downtown.
He sees lots of new things.

Bow-Wow sits in the park and sees some clowns in gowns. A big crowd claps and cheers.

Bow-Wow sniffs the red and purple flowers. He meets a brown cat.

"Howdy, Brown Cat," Bow-Wow barks. The brown cat hisses at him. Bow-Wow howls and runs.

"How did I get here?" Bow-Wow thinks. "Look at all the tall towers! Where am I?"

Now Bow-Wow starts to frown and howl. "Help! I am lost!"

"Bow-Wow!" a girl shouts. "I have found you at last!"

The Grouchy Mice

by Eva Sanchez
illustrated by Casey Craig

25

Pinky sat on her couch and called Winky. "Let's go out," she said.

"OK," said Winky.
"Let's drive downtown."

At the corner, Pinky said, "Let's turn north." Winky said, "Let's turn south."

Winky turned south. Pinky slouched down. She started to pout and mumble out loud. "What a grouch," said Winky.

When they got to town, they saw black clouds. It started to shower. Big, round drops were pounding the ground.

"This is a mess!" shouted Winky.
"Our trip isn't working out!"
"What a grouch," said Pinky.
"I think showers are nice."

Then the grouchy mice started to giggle. Friends can't be grouchy for long.

Howdy Clown

Word Count: 79

High-Frequency Words

around
doesn't
into
looks
what

Decodable Words*

a	**Howdy**	slaps
all	I	smile
and	is	smiles
bad	it	the
Clown	just	**town**
down	lips	trots
face	makes	up
feeling	need	upon
flips	**now**	upside
frown	place	while
frowns	red	yips
giggle	sad	
growls	sees	
her	she	

*Words with /ou/*ow* appear in **boldface** type.

What Joan Found
Word Count: 103

High-Frequency Words

are	some
don't	something
have	they
into	to
kind	what
of	you

Decodable Words*

a	hush	she's
and	I	**shout**
back	in	small
ball	is	**sound**
bug	it	sow
bugs	Joan	that's
crouching	like	the
curls	made	tickles
dad	make	tree
damp	**mound**	tumbles
digging	near	up
down	**round**	wet
found	rushes	whispers
gets	see	
ground	she	

*Words with /ou/*ou* appear in **boldface** type.

Bow-Wow Hound
Word Count: 102

High-Frequency Words

have	new	to
here	of	where
look	some	you

Decodable Words*

a	did	**howdy**	shouts
all	**downtown**	**howl**	sits
am	**flowers**	I	sniffs
and	found	in	starts
at	**frown**	last	tall
barks	get	lost	the
big	girl	lots	things
Bow-Wow	**gowns**	meets	thinks
brown	he	**now**	**towers**
cat	help	park	trots
cheers	him	purple	**yowls**
claps	hisses	red	
clowns	hound	runs	
crowd	**how**	sees	

*Words with /ou/*ow* appear in **boldface** type.

The Grouchy Mice

Word Count: 108

High-Frequency Words

are	said	to	working
friends	saw	were	
go	they	what	

Decodable Words*

a	for	mumble	showers
and	giggle	nice	**slouched**
at	got	north	**south**
be	**grouch**	OK	started
big	**grouchy**	on	the
black	**ground**	**our**	then
called	her	**out**	think
can't	is	Pinky	this
clouds	isn't	**pounding**	town
corner	it	**pout**	trip
couch	let's	**round**	turn
down	long	sat	turned
downtown	**loud**	she	when
drive	mess	**shouted**	Winky
drops	mice	shower	

*Words with /ou/*ou* appear in **boldface** type.